FOLLOW THE GUIDE

round the PALAIS ROHAN

STRASBOURG'S MUSEUM OF DECORATIVE ARTS

Text and illustrations by
Maryla BOUTINEAU - MABOU

English version revised by
Richard TANNER

Published by
I.D. l'Édition

My heartfelt appreciation is due to the curators of the Strasbourg Museum of Decorative Arts and to the architects of the French Historic Monuments Department, who spare neither time nor energy in the conservation of the Rohan palace.

FOREWORD

One evening last winter I attended, with a number of colleagues, a sumptuous reception held at the Rohan palace. The host was a major French firm, which had chosen the palace as a venue to assemble its employees posted across the country. As art history guides, my colleagues and I were expected to make a young, trendy, energetic gathering aware of the cultural and historical value of the palace, a prestigious building dating back to pre-Revolutionary times.

That night the Rohan palace was oblivious of its age and eagerly attuned to the happy mood of its guests. The subdued hum of conversation, the creaking of floors under stiletto heels, the bursts of laughter, the tinkle of crystal glasses, the inviting fragrance of refined dishes, all contributed powerfully to recreating the smart and witty atmosphere which had prevailed at 18th century receptions at the palace, where diplomatic issues were often at stake.

Little did it matter that these 21st century visitors were not bewigged and that the ladies wore no crinolines. A festive spirit prevailed, and the palace was fully party to it. That night the Rohan palace seemed to regain the prestige it had enjoyed at the time of prince-bishops and cardinals.

It occurred to me that evening that it would be appropriate to contribute a small publication as a token of my admiration for this jewel of the French heritage.

M.B.

In an attempt to bring 18th century moods and manners closer to today's visitors, I have enlisted the kindly help of Henriette Louise de Waldner de Freundstein, ***baronne d'Oberkirch*** *(1754-1803).*

An Alsatian protestant of noble stock, Baroness Oberkirch had perfect command of French and German and was a woman of great culture. She was friendly with Sophie Dorothée of Wurtemberg (1759-1828), who was to become Empress consort of Russia as Maria Feodorovna. (The imperial couple travelled through Europe as "Comte and Comtesse du Nord."*) This friendship gave the baroness access to the court at Versailles, where she was presented to Queen consort Marie-Antoinette, wife to King Louis XVI.*

The baroness was acquainted with the prince-bishop of Strasbourg, kept up a correspondence with Goethe, inspired Jakob Michael Reinhold Lenz (a German poet and playwright) with a true passion and admired Beaumarchais' writings. Her Memoirs are a witty and comprehensive description of the occupations and preoccupations of an aristocratic society which was casting its last sparkling rays before being caught up in the throes of the French Revolution.

PROLOGUE

Having been part of the Holy Roman Empire of the German Nation for centuries, Strasbourg was united with France in 1681 by King Louis XIV, who rewarded it with the title of Free Royal City.

A few years later Armand-Gaston de Rohan became Prince-bishop of Strasbourg. Once elected to this high office, he first chose to live in his great palace in Saverne. But, having soon realised that he needed to be present in the capital of the region, he decided to replace the former bishop's palace in Strasbourg with a splendid new residence and commissioned **Robert de Cotte**, a famous Parisian architect, to design it.

As a member of one of the major aristocratic families of France, Armand-Gaston was accustomed to the magnificence of Versailles. He therefore wanted his new palace to reflect his background and position, as well as the splendour of the French court. He also required it to provide accommodation for the king, members of the royal family and other distinguished guests, should the occasion arise.

The layout of the palace is typical of the great Parisian houses of the 18th century, with its entrance portal (gate), two pavilions, a courtyard (*cour d'honneur*), coach-houses and stable-wings. The courtyard is designed to set off the richly decorated façade of the main building. The central part of the façade overlooking the river Ill is crowned by a dome, giving it a stately appearance.

The iconographical conception of the palace, as revealed through the statues, reliefs and paintings, is emblematic of the return of catholicism to a city which had been dominated by protestantism for the previous two centuries.

Building work on the Rohan palace proceeded from 1732 until 1742 under the supervision of Joseph Massol, the city architect in charge. The palace belonged to the House of Rohan until the French Revolution, when it was confiscated, becoming the Town Hall in 1791. At that time many items of furniture and works of art in the palace were sold. In 1805 it was presented by the city to Napoleon, the newly proclaimed Emperor of the French.

From 1871 to 1918 Strasbourg was the capital of the Imperial Territory of Alsace-Lorraine – a territory created by the German Empire in 1871 after it had annexed Alsace and Moselle. The palace was used by the German university as an administrative building and library. At the very end of the 19th century it received the municipal art collections. In 1944 the palace was damaged by Allied bombing. Full restoration of the buildings was completed only in the 1990s.

Today the Rohan palace, a major architectural, historical and cultural landmark in the city, is considered a masterpiece of French classical architecture.

TABLE OF CONTENTS

THE ROHAN PALACE AND ITS APARTMENTS

COLLECTIONS OF THE MUSEUM OF DECORATIVE ARTS

THE EXTERIOR OF THE PALACE

If we start by taking a few moments to observe the exterior of the palace, it comes as a surprise to see how much it departs from the architectural style usual in Strasbourg at the time: what has become of the picturesque timbered façades and of the tile-clad sloping roofs so typical of this region?

It is as though a large section of the Palace of Versailles had detached itself from its foundations and had somehow found its way to Strasbourg, eventually settling on the bank of the River Ill a stone's throw from the medieval cathedral. After all, the Rohan palace is the only 18th century palace in Strasbourg to be quite detached from the surrounding buildings.

Until the palace had been completed, only very few people in Strasbourg understood what a genuine classical style *à la française* looked like. When the construction work came to an end in 1742, a spellbound crowd gathered outside the portal – a solemn and imposing gate reminiscent of a triumphal arch. For the common people everything was new in this vast building – the female statues with well-rounded shapes, the groups of plump cherubs playing with a cardinal's hat or a bishop's crozier, the high reliefs standing for Justice and Charity. They would gaze at the keystone masks over the windows, displaying Old Testament patriarchs, prophets and heroes such as **Moses**, Aaron, Myriam, the **prophetess Ann** or **King David**.

They would gape at the lions and the elephants, which struck a novel note as ornamental items on the walls.

Group of angels symbolizing the function of the Bishop

Group of cherubs symbolizing the function of the Cardinal

Group of cherubs symbolizing the Holy Communion

Hercules

The frontage on the river Ill is larger, higher and more ornate than the one facing the courtyard. The central part of this façade is crowned by a dome.

Moses

The prophetess Anna

King David

The crowds that flocked to the palace were thrilled by the heads of spirited steeds decorating the servants' quarters. On the other hand, it might be difficult for the common man to put a name to the deities strung out along the façade overlooking the river. He might hesitate between Jupiter, Juno, Neptune, Mars, Minerva, Ceres and **Hercules**.

The downward-facing young woman representing **Religion**, below the balcony of the library, was found particularly engaging. Young men dreamt of the young ladies whose pretty faces enlivened the façade under the French-style balconies.

Religion

The people of Strasbourg were dazzled by the beauty of the palace; these men and women, usually shunning unnecessary expense, forgot overnight that for two centuries they had been subject to protestant thriftiness. The sheer appeal of the palace prompted them to build their own homes in the new fashionable "French" style. In the wake of this architectural renewal experienced by the city in the 18th century, there sprung up a number of houses built of dressed stone. They had "French" balconies with ornate wrought-iron structures and windows topped with carved **mascarons.** The rococo doors and gates with their "gingerbread" design say a lot about the readiness, indeed the enthusiasm, of the Strasbourg people to adopt the features of French architecture. Those who could not afford such a costly change of style at least made a point of applying a rendering layer over their timbered façades.

*A **mascaron** ornament is a face, usually a human face. In the 18th century it often represented an Antique god, a season, a continent or a frame of mind.*

The entrance gate is surmounted by two allegorical groups representing **Religion** and **Clemency**.

Explanatory notes

The terms in bold text are explained in the notes in italics placed alongside the main text. They may also be illustrated by a drawing.

Religion

Clemency

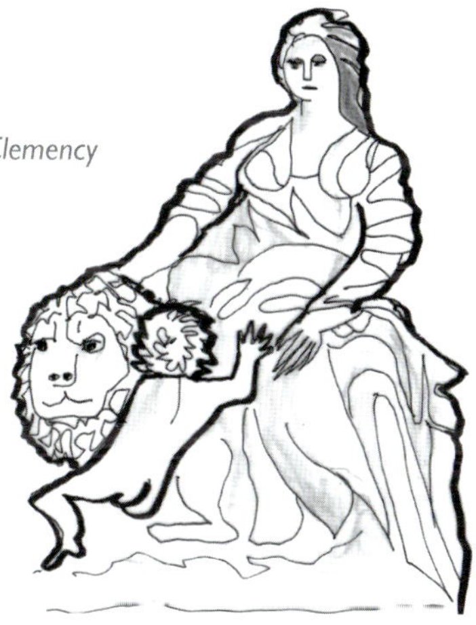

The author of the architectural project was ***Robert de Cotte*** *(1656-1735). A French architect and urban planner, he was one of the most influential rococo designers. He promoted French architecture throughout Europe, notably in the German-speaking lands. In 1708 he became "Chief Architect to the King". He designed bishop's palaces in Châlons-sur-Marne, Verdun and Strasbourg, while Joseph Massol (1706-1771) supervised the construction.*

THE MAIN COURTYARD

Our short walk around the palace brings us in front of the main portal, whose richly carved oak wings open into an oblong courtyard lined on one side by an elegant façade featuring nine windows.

The prominent central section is crowned with a classical triangular pediment with two cherubs proudly displaying the coat of arms of Armand-Gaston de Rohan. Two female figures reclining on the pediment dominate the courtyard. They personify the virtues of **Fortitude** and **Prudence.**

The façade is flanked to the right and left by vestibules, the one to the left housing the main entrance. The vestibule at the right end houses the servants' entrance, but is just as ornate as the main one in order to create that illusion of symmetry which is so important in classical French architecture.

Le sanguin

Melancholic

Choleric

Fortitude

Prudence

The four male heads over the windows of the main courtyard probably represent different tempers – **choleric**, "*le* ***sanguin***", **melancholic**, **phlegmatic**. The women may personify the four **continents**. The centre of the façade is occupied by the **jester.**

Phlegmatic

The jester

Asia

The goddess Flora

THE SYNOD HALL, INCLUDING THE DINING HALL AND GUARDROOM

Walking past the grand staircase with its ornate wrought-iron banisters, we greet the charming **goddess Flora**, before entering the Synod hall, a huge space flooded with light. The Synod hall with its ten windows extends right across the depth of the building. The two white-tiled stoves placed against the wall are replicas of stoves used in bygone days to keep out the cold, which could be severe. Today they perform a purely aesthetic function.

Walnut chairs – modern copies of those sold during the French Revolution – are lined up along the wall. The brightness of this hall is enhanced by the white walls and the pale Italian-style curtains. The original sandstone floor was replaced by **Comblanchien** stone after the Second World War.

Comblanchien is a town in the Burgundy-Franche-Comté region, where a type of limestone as hard as marble is still quarried today.

A row of arches divides the Synod hall into two parts – the dining hall and the guardroom. The arches are decorated with sculpted bronze-coloured **trophies**, which display the ingredients of a fine banquet – game and fish, wine, fruit, water – plus a **theatrical mask** and musical instruments. Four trophies represent the Four Times of Day in allegorical fashion.

Theatrical mask

On the subject of **hunting, theatre and music**, Baroness Oberkirch wrote:

"After the music there was a walk, and in the evening a hunt by torchlight. All the ladies were in open carriages, the princesses together, whilst the gentlemen rode alongside. The stags ran terrified by the light of the torches, the pack followed barking: the effect it produced in such a setting was fairy-like…"

"…The Barber of Seville – that cornerstone of the edifice raised against the nobility by Beaumarchais. We all applauded the satire against ourselves; we all approved and blessed the weapons that were later to wound us…"

"The harp was just then coming into fashion and many ladies saw it only as an opportunity of displaying their lovely arms and beautiful feet, besides which the attitude of the performer was very graceful."

"The countess du Nord showed me a ballad and a rondo for the harpsichord which had been presented to her the same morning by the composer…"

"After dinner the entire court assembled in the salon de la paix, *where there was to be a concert…A thousand chandeliers depended from the ceilings, and every bracket supported a branch holding forty wax-lights…"*

Trophy

*The **theatrical mask** might seem surprising in an ecclesiastical palace, but for the fact that in the 18th century society as a whole was infatuated with dramatic art. Voltaire wrote tragedies, Diderot invented the "drama" as a genre; Marivaux and Beaumarchais wrote witty, sophisticated comedies which showed great psychological insight. Queen Marie-Antoinette herself acted on stage for her close friends in her small private theatre.*

THE DINING HALL

In the dining hall we can still admire the original decorative feature against the northern wall – a pair of baroque basins which would be filled with water before a banquet took place. Above the red of the **Rance marble** basins, two young water divinities in bronze-coloured **stucco** play with dolphins and swans against a fairy-tale landscape.

The dining hall could seat up to three hundred guests.

Internal ***stucco****, widely used in the 18th century, was made of very fine sand with powdered Carrara marble, gypsum, alabaster dust, fat lime and water. It was often gilded.*

Rance marble *has a brownish-red colour, veined with white and blue. It originates from Rance in the Belgian province of Hainaut. A prestigious building material for decorative purposes, it was abundantly used in the Royal Palace of Versailles, including its Hall of Mirrors. Rance marble was quarried well into the 1950s.*

Water divinity

In the 18th century, to accommodate dozens of guests the dining table was assembled with trestles and wooden planks and covered with a tablecloth. The tableware was as fine as possible and in the middle of the table was placed the decorative centrepiece made of silver, vermeil (silver-gilt), crystal or fine earthenware.

Standing on a credence-table, a bust of **Julius Caesar** crowned with laurel contemplates the hall. It once belonged to **Cardinal Mazarin**. Between the basins, a *trompe-l'œil* painting of Ceres, the harvest goddess, holds a sickle in one hand and a sheaf of wheat ears in the other.

The kitchens occupy one of the pavilions on the other side of the courtyard, quite a long way from the apartments to ensure that neither fire nor smells can reach the main residential part.

Ceres

Two guests holding glasses in an 18th century pose

Julius Caesar
(100 B.C. - 44 B.C.), was a statesman, writer and general. A great strategist and cunning tactician, he extended Rome's territory to the English Channel and the Rhine. Caesar's military victories put him in an unrivalled position of power and influence. After assuming control of the government, Caesar was proclaimed "dictator in perpetuity" but soon after was assassinated by a group of senators led by Marcus Junius Brutus, his adopted son. Caesar is considered one of the greatest military commanders in history. From the end of the 1st century onwards the Augustus VIII Legion, created by Julius Caesar, was stationed in Strasbourg, which the Romans called Argentoratum.

Jules-Raymond Mazarin *(1602-1661), was an Italian-born cardinal, diplomat and politician. When King Louis XIII died in 1643, his successor Louis XIV was only five years old. His mother, Anne of Austria, ruled in his place until he came of age. Mazarin ruled France jointly with the queen during her regency, and until his death he was a passionate art and jewel collector. Some items of his collection were later purchased by Armand-Gaston de Rohan and are today exhibited in this museum. The famed Mazarin Library in Paris ("la Mazarine") has its origin in Cardinal Mazarin's personal library.*

On the subject of table arrangements, Baroness Oberkirch wrote:

"The supper was laid out on several small tables, as was the custom at Trianon and Chantilly, a fashion that is far more social and convenient than those long tables at which one can never feel so much at ease."

Until the 17th century the French diet consisted chiefly of spicy boiled meats, for those who could afford them. No health benefits were expected of vegetables. Under Louis XIV a change occurred. The king himself loved his garden and the fruit and vegetables it produced, and thus began the process that was to bring French cuisine to the summit.

The 17th century saw the appearance of French chefs who codified and modernized French cuisine: François-Pierre La Varenne (1615-1678), Nicolas Bonnefons and François Massialot (1660-1733).

La Varenne described French cuisine as "*delicately prepared*" and advocated that plates be garnished with flowers. He introduced the first *bisque, hollandaise sauce* and *béchamel sauce*. He replaced lard with butter and breadcrumbs with *roux* as the base for sauces. His *duxelles* – a finely minced mushroom mixture – became the favourite flavouring for fish and vegetables. His *millefeuille* soon became famous. He also created jams, jellies, syrups, compotes and a wide variety of fruit drinks. To Bonnefons we owe conserves, dried fruit, jellies, fruit spread, marzipan and macaroons. As for Massialot, he earned a reputation for his *marinade* and his *ragoût*, but also his *meringue*, *crème brûlée*, chocolate cream and custard cream.

At that time vegetables like cauliflower, asparagus, peas, cucumber and artichoke were introduced. Truffles, morels, crayfish, skylark *pâté*, turtle stew, cockscombs were considered delicacies. Transport improvements led to higher expectations concerning the freshness of fish. Salty dishes were henceforth kept strictly separate from sweet ones.

Sugar was a luxury in Europe until the 18th century, when it became more widely available. The introduction of sugar into European cookery resulted in a large variety of new pastry recipes. The sugar was produced in sugarcane plantations in the Caribbean (French West Indies – Martinique, Guadeloupe and Saint-Domingue).

In 1780 Alsatian *foie gras* was created by Jean-Pierre Clause (1757-1827), cook to Louis-Georges Erasme, marquis de Contades (1704-1795), military commander of Strasbourg.

Thanks to the skills of Dom Pérignon (1638-1715), champagne became a must on aristocratic tables. Chocolate, coffee and tea became highly fashionable beverages. In the wine cellars of the Rohan palace were stored bottles of Burgundy, Moselle, Champagne, Spanish and Alsatian wine.

The mineral appearance of the hall is softened by the decorative compositions of **Jean-Baptiste Oudry** depicting such aristocratic pleasures as hunting, music and literature. The prince-bishop of Strasbourg himself had a hunting lodge in Mutzig and a magnificent library in Strasbourg.

Jean-Baptiste Oudry *(1686-1755) was a French rococo painter, engraver and tapestry designer. He is known for his naturalistic pictures of animals and his hunt pieces depicting game. He was director of the Beauvais tapestry works. He made a series of tapestry cartoons depicting "Pastoral Amusements", and also painted Louis XV hunting deer in Saint-Germain forest.*

Two monumental blue and white lidded jars of the Qing dynasty (early 18th century) stand on the Louis XIV consoles. They belonged to the **far-eastern decorative art collection** of prince-bishop Louis de Rohan.

The far-eastern collection of Louis de Rohan

Prince-bishop Louis de Rohan was infatuated with the Far East. His outstanding collection of "chinoiseries", which used to be in the Saverne Palace – his country residence – consisted of all sorts of vases of sometimes impressive size, with jars, basins, dragons, Chinese lacquerware, reverse glass paintings and porcelain pagodas. Today many items in this collection are on display in the palace apartments.

The plump **cherubs** of the **overdoors** mime scenes which symbolize the four seasons and the four elements – water, air, earth and fire.

Cherubs – symbolizing autumn

Leaving the guardroom, we proceed to the king's apartment, consisting of three rooms – an antechamber, the king's bedchamber and the assembly hall. The king's apartment overlooks the river Ill, while the private quarters of the prince-bishop overlook the "***cour d'honneur***" (main courtyard). Each apartment forms an "***enfilade***" of adjoining rooms.

An ***overdoor*** *is a painting,* bas-relief *(low relief) or decorative panel set within ornamental mouldings over a door. Overdoor paintings, considered as a minor genre of their own, were often trompe-l'oeil representations of stone reliefs, vases of flowers, allegorical subjects, landscapes or animals.*

Cour d'honneur *(main courtyard) is the architectural term for a three-sided courtyard; the corps de logis (main central block) is flanked by symmetrically advancing secondary wings housing the servants'quarters.* The cour d'honneur *forms the ceremonial entrance to the building.*

An **enfilade** *is a suite of rooms along the same axis. Leaving the doors open creates a stunning perspective.*

THE KING'S ANTECHAMBER

also called THE BISHOPS' HALL

Parquet de Versailles
is a geometric mosaic of wood pieces used for decorative effect. Large diagonal squares, known as "parquet de Versailles", were introduced in 1684 as wooden parquet to replace the marble flooring in the Palace of Versailles and the Grand Trianon. It afforded more efficient thermal insulation than the marble floor.

Note the difference between the mineral appearance of the guardroom and the king's antechamber. While the decoration remains sober, the atmosphere is warmed by four things: the off-white wooden panelling (as opposed to stucco) on the walls; the gilded elements which adorn the walls (including the coats-of-arms of the German prince-bishops who were Armand Gaston's predecessors); the crimson curtains; and, last but not least, the wooden parquetry (***parquet de Versailles)***. The four corners of the ceiling display the **monogram** of Armand-Gaston de Rohan.

In the centre of the ceiling the Cross of the ***Ordre du Saint-Esprit*** reminds us that Armand-Gaston de Rohan was the commander of that Order.

The **Ordre du Saint-Esprit** *(Order of the Holy Spirit or Holy Ghost) was the highest order of chivalry under the French monarchy. It was created in 1578 by Henri III and was reserved for princes and powerful nobles. It was officially abolished in 1830.*

The full-length portrait of Armand-Gaston de Rohan – a copy of an original by ***Hyacinthe Rigaud*** *– has been replaced by a modern copy. The effigy of the prince-bishop on the wall opposite the door gives visitors a solemn welcome. Armand-Gaston sat for Rigaud in 1710 at the age of 36.*

The **monogram** of Armand Gaston de Rohan

Hyacinthe Rigaud
(1659-1743) was a French painter of Catalan origin who arrived in Paris in 1681. He was one of the major portrait painters during the reign of Louis XIV. His instinct for grand presentation suited the tastes of the monarchs, princes, ambassadors, clerics, courtiers and financiers who sat for him. Rigaud received staunch support from the four generations of Bourbons whose portraits he painted. His œuvre can be viewed as a near-complete portrait gallery of the main personages of high society in France from 1680 to 1740.

Joseph Melling
(1724 -1796) was a Lorraine-born painter who studied in Paris with Carle van Loo and François Boucher. He worked as court painter at Karlsruhe palace before settling in Strasbourg in 1774 and producing historical and religious paintings.

The portraits of Armand-Gaston de Rohan and his German predecessors decorated the walls for about fifty years. In 1793, at the peak of the French Revolution, they were burnt and replaced by the civic virtues of **Joseph Melling** – Prudence, Peace, Immortality, Civil Harmony, Zeal and Public Felicity. For a few years these virtues presided over the meetings of the city council, at a time when the palace served as Town Hall. In 1805 the palace was offered to the Emperor Napoleon for his personal use.

The ***Empire style*** *is a neo-classical style of decoration and interior design that evolved in the Napoleonic period in France during the first fifteen years of the 19th century. It drew on Egyptian, Greek, Etruscan, Pompeian and Roman motifs. After Napoleon lost power, the Empire style continued to find favour for many decades.*

Porcelain *(china) is a ceramic product made by heating materials in a kiln to temperatures between 1,200 and 1,400 °C (2,200 and 2,600 °F). Kaolin, together with feldspar and quartz, is the primary material from which porcelain is made. Porcelain may be described as being hard, impermeable, white, translucent and resonant. It originated in China, where it was developed from the ceramic wares used during the Eastern Han dynasty (206 B.C.-220 A.D.). In Europe, porcelain was first produced in Dresden in 1708.*

The combined monogram of Napoleon and Josephine, together with the imperial eagle, remind us that the couple spent a while in the palace.

The **Empire style** pier tables between the windows bear witness to Napoleon's wish to refurnish the palace after the furniture had been dispersed during the Revolution.

Four blue and white Chinese **porcelain** cylinder vases (Qing dynasty, Kangxi period 1662-1722) of impressive size stand on the pier tables between the windows. They are adorned with flowers, landscapes and precious objects.

Each pair of blue and white vases surrounds a *famille verte* cylinder vase (Qing Dynasty, Kangxi period 1662-1722). Their surface is alive with images of refined young ladies chatting with friends in a secluded setting, while their children play under the caring gaze of the servants, and other scenes from the everyday life of Chinese high society.

On the large console table dating from 1740 is displayed the *garniture*, which consists of three octagonal lidded jars and two beaker-shaped cornet vases. This Japanese *garniture* dates from the 18th century.

Cornet vase

Octagonal lidded jar

***Caligula** (12 A.D.-41 A.D.)*
Roman emperor (37 A.D.-41 A.D.)

***Nero** (37 A.D. - 68 A.D.)*
Roman emperor (54 A.D.- 68 A.D.)

***Trajan** (53 A.D.-117 A.D.)*
Roman emperor (98 A.D.-117 A.D.)

***Antoninus Pius** (86 A.D.-161 A.D.)*
Roman emperor (138 A.D. -161 A.D.)

Marcus Aurelius
(121 A.D. -180 A.D.)
Roman emperor (161 A.D. -180 A.D.)

***Lucius Verus** (130 A.D.-169 A.D.)*
Roman co-emperor with Marcus Aurelius (161 A.D.-169 A.D.)

Septimius Severus
(145 A.D. - 211 A.D.)
Roman emperor (193 A.D. -211 A.D.)

The **busts of Roman Emperors** are copies of antique ones. The copies, sculpted in the 17th century, belonged to Cardinal Mazarin. Prince-bishop Armand-Gaston de Rohan bought them from his niece, who had inherited Mazarin's collection.

In the 18th century there were plenty of benches, armchairs, cane chairs and stools here. The antechamber served mainly as a gaming-room.

Today a few pieces of furniture hark back to the original 18th century baize-covered card tables. The players indulged their passion under the gaze of seven Roman emperors – **Caligula**, **Nero**, **Trajan**, **Antoninus Pius**, **Marcus Aurelius**, **Lucius Verus** and **Septimius Severus** (two busts). No doubt these marble emperors could entertain us with tales of bewigged cheats and their willing victims.

Louis-César-Constantin, Prince of Rohan (1697-1779).

Early in life he took up a military career. After serving as knight of the Order of Saint John of Jerusalem (Order of Malta), he served as a commissioned officer in the royal navy, where he was promoted to captain in 1720. He was 35 when he left the navy for the Church and was appointed canon and provost marshall of Strasbourg Cathedral. In 1748 he was appointed first almoner. In 1753 he was made commander of the Order of the Holy Spirit. In 1756, after the death of François-Armand de Rohan, he became prince-bishop of Strasbourg and landgrave of Alsace. He was made a cardinal by Pope Clement XIII in 1761.

Louis-René-Édouard, Prince of Rohan (1734-1803).

A grand-nephew of Louis-César-Constantin, Louis-René-Edouard found himself canon of the cathedral at the age of 9. In 1761, at the age of 27, this clergyman, philosopher and poet, a friend of Buffon and d'Alembert, was elected to the *Académie française*. Ten years later he became ambassador in Vienna, where Empress Maria Theresa, Marie-Antoinette's mother, did not greatly appreciate him. Back in France in 1777, he was appointed Grand Almoner of France. Queen Marie-Antoinette disliked him as much as her mother did. In 1779 he replaced his great-uncle in the see of Strasbourg. Later he became chief administrator of the Sorbonne. In 1785 his status was shattered by the Diamond Necklace scandal (the notorious "*affaire du Collier*"). Louis-René-Edouard died in Ettenheim, Baden-Württemberg, the German part of his diocese.

The **Affair of the diamond necklace** was an incident which took place in 1785 at the court of Louis XVI. It can be briefly recounted as follows.

In 1772 King Louis XV decided to present Madame du Barry, his mistress, with a diamond necklace of exceptional value. The necklace consisted of many large diamonds arranged in an elaborate design. Parisian jewellers Boehmer and Bassenge, who were commissioned to create it, took several years to assemble an appropriate set of diamonds. In the meantime, Louis XV died and Madame du Barry was banished from court by Louis XVI. The jewellers attempted to sell the necklace to Marie-Antoinette, but she refused.

The diamond necklace

An imposter known as Jeanne de la Motte conceived a plan to use the necklace to gain wealth and power. At that time, Cardinal Louis-René de Rohan wanted to regain Marie-Antoinette's goodwill. Jeanne persuaded him that she enjoyed the favour of the queen and could help him to that end. Together with her husband and other accomplices she forged several letters signed "*Marie-Antoinette de France*", addressed to the cardinal. She even arranged a nightly secret assignation in the park of Versailles between the prelate and a prostitute whom he took for the queen.

Jeanne told the cardinal that Marie-Antoinette wanted him to act as a secret intermediary in purchasing the necklace. Rohan negotiated its purchase for 2,000,000 livres, to be paid in instalments, and took it to Jeanne's house, where a man whom Rohan believed to be a valet to the queen came to collect it. Jeanne's husband secretly took the necklace to London, where it was broken up in order for the large individual diamonds to be sold separately.

When the time came to pay up, the queen told Boehmer that she had neither ordered nor received the necklace. Rohan was arrested and taken to the Bastille. A sensational trial followed, resulting in the acquittal of the cardinal, who was exiled to the Abbey of la Chaise-Dieu. Jeanne de la Motte was condemned to be whipped, branded with a V (for "*voleuse*", i.e. "thief") and imprisoned for life; but after a few months she managed to escape to London. She died in a fall from her hotel room window.

Public opinion was greatly excited by this trial. The affair of the diamond necklace was important in discrediting the Bourbon monarchy in the eyes of the French people. The queen's reputation was ruined by this affair, as she was suspected of implication in a crime of fraud. The affair, among other causes, eventually culminated in the French Revolution. However, historians generally conclude that Marie-Antoinette was blameless in the matter and that Rohan was an innocent dupe, deceived by the La Motte couple.

Giuseppe Balsamo (1743-1795) called himself Count Alessandro di ***Cagliostro***

Of Italian origin, Cagliostro was one of the famous occultists, adventurers, magicians, healers and alchimists who haunted the aristocratic courts of Europe in the 18th century. He became a glamorous figure and had many followers in high society circles. In 1780 Cagliostro settled with his pretty young wife Serafina for some time in Strasbourg at 7, rue des Ecrivains, close to the Rohan Palace. The prince-bishop considered him a superior being. He installed a laboratory for him under the palace roof, hoping that Cagliostro would supply him with fresh gold. Beside his other activities, Cagliostro was active in the spread of freemasonry. He introduced the acceptance of women into the community.

In 1785 he followed the prince-bishop of Rohan to Paris. Soon after, the glittering coaches of his admirers were queueing in front of his mansion… After the Affair of the diamond necklace broke, he was held in the Bastille for nine months, but was finally acquitted when no evidence was found connecting him to the affair. When at last he emerged from prison, his enthusiastic followers carried him triumphantly home. Nonetheless, he was asked to leave France, and went to London. He had the ill-timed idea to visit Rome, where he was arrested and imprisoned in Castel Sant'Angelo. He was sentenced to death by the Inquisition on the charge of freemasonry. The Pope commuted his sentence to life imprisonment, but Cagliostro died shortly afterwards in the fortress of San Leo.

About **prince-bishop Louis-René-Edouard de Rohan** Baroness Oberkirch wrote:

"The dauphin was baptized on the day following his birth by the Cardinal Prince de Rohan, Grand Almoner and Bishop of Strasbourg."
" …the Prince de Rohan, Bishop of Strasbourg…was very courteous to us, though we were not of his flock. "
"The Bishop is a very handsome man, in whose devotion there is nothing ascetic, and who has no objection to the society of ladies."
"Though endowed with high intelligence and possessing amiable manners, extreme credulity led him into weaknesses, which he has expiated in deep sorrow, and which have cost our poor Queen many a bitter tear in the vexatious history of the necklace."

About **Cagliostro** Baroness Oberkirch wrote:

"We found the whole town busy talking about a charlatan, who has since become very famous, and who was then commencing a system of trickery which has since enabled him to play so extraordinary a part."
"I cannot deny that Cagliostro possessed an almost demoniacal power; he fascinated the mind."

About **the relationship between the prince-bishop and Cagliostro**, Baroness Oberkirch wrote:

"The Cardinal said : Cagliostro can make gold! (...) He will make me the richest prince in Europe."

Seraphina and Alessandro di Cagliostro

THE KING'S BEDCHAMBER

The king's bedchamber is the most important room of the royal apartments. It is entirely panelled with oak, painted a neutral light grey to enhance the gilt ornaments adorning the walls.

Mask of a man with a feather headdress

Sunflowers – the Rohans'emblematic flowers – are incorporated into the decoration

Exuberant stucco, wood or metal shapes invade the room. Poppies climb up the pier-glass; the slender body of a hound facing a wild boar is entangled in the swirls of a **wall light**; the corners of the ceiling are inhabited by Aurora, Venus, Diana and Proserpina – the deities symbolizing morning, noon, evening and night. Winged sphinxes with clawed feet and feather hairdress seem to ensure their safety. In the middle of the cornice moulding, a **man wearing a nightcap** looks down at a **yawning mascaron**. **Female figures** with tiny wings try to squeeze out of the intricate frames of the overdoors. **Men with feather headdress** watch over the canopied bed. All these people of the shadows watch over the "crowned sleepers" who pass through the Rohan palace (unless they give them nightmares!).

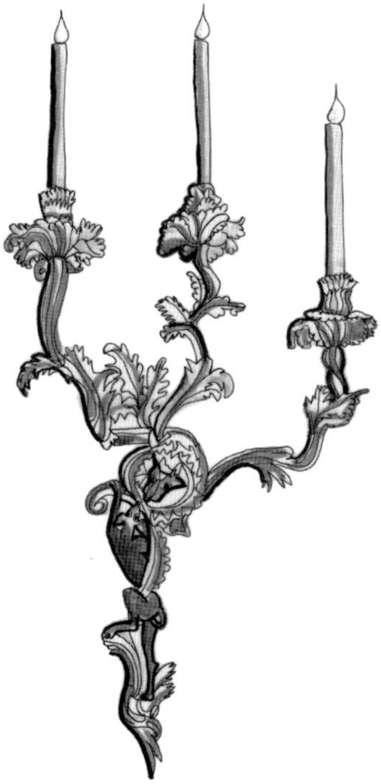

Wall-light with hound and wild boar

Female figure in the frame of an overdoor

Man in a nightcap and yawning mascaron

The overdoors feature copies by **Pierre-Ignace Parrocel** of the original paintings by **Raphaël** which are to be seen in the loggias of the Vatican: **David anointed by Samuel**, **Solomon and the Queen of Sheba**, **Abraham and Melchizedek** and the **Baptism of Christ**.

Abraham and Melchizedek

David anointed by Samuel

Solomon and the Queen of Sheba (detail)

Abraham and Melchizedek

Abraham in armour surrounded by his soldiers embodies temporal power; Melchizedek, among his servants with amphoras full of wine and baskets of bread, stands for spiritual power.

David anointed by Samuel

Samuel is shown advanced in years. He solemnly pours oil on the head of a very young David, dressed in shepherd's clothing and holding his shepherd's crook. David's seven brothers are present, and so is his father Jesse.

Solomon and the Queen of Sheba

The Queen of Sheba, a woman famous for her beauty, is mentioned in the stories of all three monotheistic religions. She arrived at Jerusalem with a numerous retinue and "camels bearing spices and gold in abundance, and precious stones." She came "to test him with hard questions", all of which Solomon answered to her satisfaction. They exchanged gifts, whereupon she returned to her own country.

The Baptism of Christ

Jesus is being baptised in the River Jordan by Saint John the Baptist.

*The encounter between **Jesus and the Samaritan** woman took place when Jesus was resting at a well. He asked the woman to give him a drink, and talked to her about God.*

*The **Temptation of Christ***

After being baptized by John the Baptist, Jesus fasted for forty days and nights in the Judaean desert. During this time Satan tried to tempt him, but Jesus warded off each attempt.

*Raffaello Sanzio da Urbino, known as **Raphael** (1483-1520), was an Italian painter and architect of the High Renaissance. His work is admired for its clarity of form, ease of composition and gracefulness.*

***Pierre-Ignace Parrocel** (1702-1775) was a painter in the service of prince-bishop Armand-Gaston de Rohan. From 1734 to 1740 he stayed in Rome and produced copies of celebrated works by famous artists.*

*The **Marriage of Constantine** features a double marriage celebrated during the period of the tetrarchy. The tetrarchy lasted until ca. 313 A.D., when most of the claimants to power were eliminated, leaving Constantine in control of the western half of the empire, and Licinius in control of the eastern half. However, Constantine had Licinius executed in 325 A.D.*

The tapestry depicts Constantine marrying Fausta, daughter of the emperor Maximian, and giving away his half-sister Constantia to the emperor Licinius, his collegue and rival. On the tapestry they are represented from left to right as follows: Fausta, her father Maximian, Constantine, Constantia and Licinius.

Two original paintings by **Pierre-Ignace Parrocel** hang above the mirrors opposite the alcove; they depict two episodes from the New Testament: **Jesus and the Samaritan woman** and the **Temptation of Christ.**

Jesus and the Samaritan woman

The canopied bed stands on a platform in an alcove. It is protected and set off by a gilt balustrade, columns and pilasters, a remarkable structure that cannot fail to draw the visitor's eye. Three tapestries belonging to The **History of Constantine** set are displayed on the rear wall of the alcove, from left to right: The **Trophy of Constantine**, The **Marriage of Constantine** and The **Labarum**.

The **Trophy of Constantine**

The emperor Constantine is crowned by a winged Victory after Maxentius' defeat. He stands in front of a collection of implements of war. Two bound captives are lying at his feet.

The ***History of Constantine*** *is a series of tapestries designed by Peter Paul Rubens, depicting the life of the emperor Constantine (272 A.D. - 337 A.D.), the first Christian emperor of Ancient Rome. In 1622 Rubens painted the oil sketches that served as guides, while the tapestries themselves were woven in the Faubourg Saint-Marcel in Paris around 1625, transforming each small sketch into a sumptuous creation of wool, silk, and gold and silver thread. The tapestries formed part of Cardinal Mazarin's collection before Armand-Gaston de Rohan acquired them.*

The **Labarum**
was a military standard displaying the monogram of Christ. The emperor Constantine presented his troops with the Labarum moments before the battle at Milvian Bridge. Confident that the day will be his, he already wears a victor's laurels on his head.

Porcelain basin with famille verte decoration

On the large console table in the Regency style (1720-30) are a pair of terracotta **Buddhist lions** (Qing dynasty) and a **porcelain basin** with *famille verte* decoration (Qing dynasty, Kangxi period, 1662-1722). The Chinese **lacquer** box dates from the same period.

The **balustrade**, the three armchairs, the six **folding stools**, the two **console tables** between the windows, the fire screen in gilded wood and the chandelier all date from the Louis XV period, ca. 1740.

Buddhist lion (detail)

Balustrade with vase-shaped balusters

Folding stool

***Lacquer** is a varnish applied in successive coats to metal or wood, used in an important branch of decorative art. Lacquer in China and Japan is made from the sap of the Chinese lacquer tree, which can be used in its natural state.*

*A 18th century **console table** is a shelflike table attached to, or leaning against, a wall. It is an important decorative element made of lavishly carved gilded wood with a marble top. Its scroll legs are often bracket-shaped.*

Console table

*The **pier-glass** is a mirror set on the wall between two windows, above a console table or on the wall above a mantelpiece. It is usually long and tall in shape in order to fit the space. Beautifully framed pier-glasses were typical decorative features in the reception rooms of 18th century palaces. Jean-Baptiste Colbert, French minister of finance (1619-1683), established the Royal Mirror-Glass Factory in 1665. Thanks to Venetian glassworkers whom he enticed to Paris, the first flawless mirrors were produced in 1666. In 1678, the company produced the glass for the Hall of Mirrors at the Palace of Versailles.*

*Quarries situated in **Sarrancolin**, a village in the high Pyrenees, were worked extensively during the reign of Louis XIV, and from 1692 were even called "royal quarries". The Sarrancolin marbles feature red flame patterns.*

*A **fire screen** was placed in front of a fireplace to keep flying sparks or hot embers away from the room. It was an important decorative element in the 18th century.*

The king's bedchamber was heated by a fireplace with a **Sarrancolin** marble mantel, in front of which a **fire screen** was placed.

On the subject of **fashion**, Baroness Oberkirch wrote:

"The baronesses wore high plumes upon their heads, a style of coiffure which suits only tall women; the chins of the smaller ladies appeared midway between their feet and the tips of these nodding plumes."

"I tried a new fashion. I wore in my hair little flat bottles shaped to the curvature of the head; into these a little water was poured, for the purpose of preserving the freshness of the natural flowers worn in the hair, and whose stems were immersed in the liquid…The effect was charming. Nothing could be more lovely than the floral wreath crowning the snowy pyramid of powdered hair."

"The Countess du Nord wore upon her head a little bird made of precious stones, so brilliant that no eye could gaze on it steadily. It was fixed upon a spring; the slightest movement of the wearer set it in motion, whereupon it fluttered its wings above the rose on which it seemed to be perched. The Queen admired it so much that she ordered a similar one for herself."

"Deprive France, and especially its capital, of its luxury, and you will deprive it of a large portion of its commercial wealth…you will deprive it of its influence in Europe…if the fashions did not come from Paris, where should they come from?"

"We were obliged to make a grand toilette. The Countess du Nord produced a great sensation both by her beauty and her magnificent dress. She wore that day a robe that had just been sent her from Paris by Mlle Bertin, it was of lace interwoven with gold, and worn over a slip of silk brocaded with velvet flowers."

"I find pearls far more becoming to the complexion than diamonds; and the ladies in the time of Louis XIV, who were learned in everything related to the toilette, never wore any ornaments but pearls, as may be seen from their portraits by Mignard."

Prominent guests who stayed at the Rohan palace

1744: Louis XV (1710-1774) at age 34. The celebrations on this occasion lasted one week.

1747: Archduchess Maria Josepha of Saxony (1731-1767) at age 15. She was to become the mother of Louis XVI, Louis XVIII and Charles X.

1770: Archduchess Marie-Antoinette at age 14, on her way to marry the Dauphin (the future King Louis XVI). Water jousting and fireworks were staged in her honour.

1805: The Emperor Napoleon (1769-1821) with Empress Josephine (1763-1814). After Napoleon had embarked on a campaign which was to reward him with a glorious victory at Austerlitz, Josephine remained by herself in the palace, where she made a point of organizing festive events for the population.

1805: Talleyrand (1754-1838), Napoleon's foreign minister. He was accompanying the emperor.

1807: Princess Catharina of Württemberg (1783-1835), after her marriage by proxy to Jerôme Bonaparte, a brother of Napoleon.

1809: Joséphine came for a second stay, during which festivities were organized in her honour in the Orangerie pavilion.

1809: Hortense de Beauharnais (1783-1837), Queen of Holland, daughter of Joséphine. Stéphanie de Beauharnais (1789-1860), Grand-Duchess of Baden, niece of Joséphine. Catharina of Württemberg, Queen of Westphalia, sister-in-law of Joséphine.

1810: Archduchess Marie-Louise of Austria (1791-1847) at age 19. She had married Napoleon by proxy; she spent her first night on French territory in this palace.

1828: Charles X (1757-1836), King of France and Navarre.

1831: Louis-Philippe (1773-1850), King of the French.

Louis XV

Maria Josepha of Saxony

Marie-Antoinette

Engraving from the collection "Fêtes données par la Ville de Strasbourg pour la convalescence du roi" *(Celebrations organized by the City of Strasbourg on the occasion of the convalescence of the King), hand-drawn by Jean-Martin Weis, engraved by Jacques-Philippe Le Bas.* (Strasbourg, Cabinet des Estampes et des Dessins)

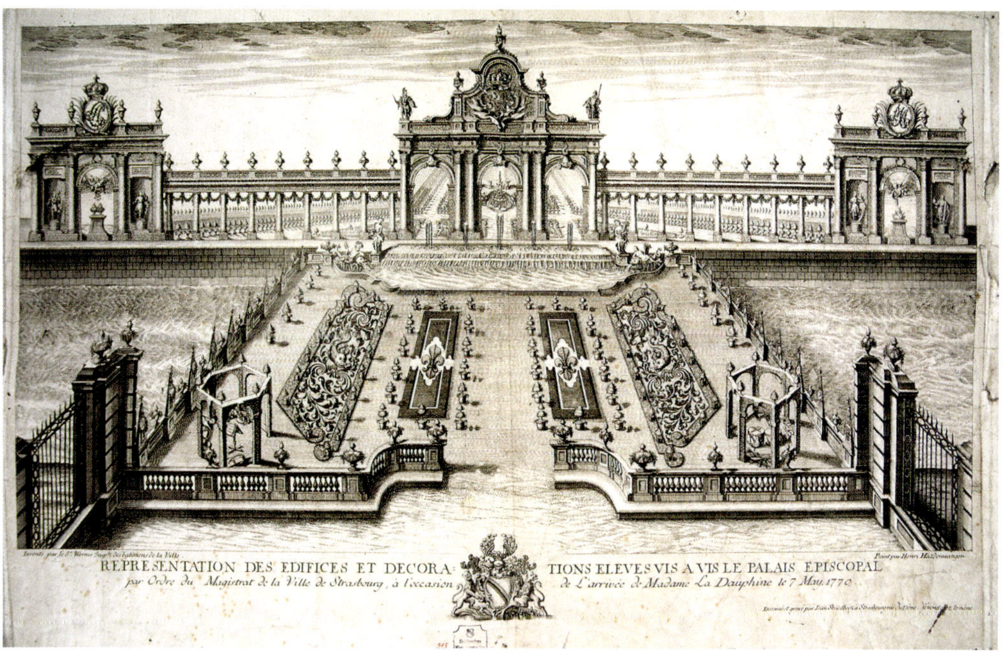

Temporary decoration placed opposite the palace façade overlooking the river during Marie-Antoinette's stay in Strasbourg in 1770. Engraved by Jean Striedbeck. (Strasbourg, Cabinet des Estampes et des Dessins)

At the age of 16, Baroness Oberkirch witnessed **the arrival of Marie-Antoinette**, Archduchess of Austria. Describing the festivities, the Baroness wrote:

"...The Dauphine, now Queen of France, passed through Strasbourg, where I went with my father to pay her our respects. Oh! if I lived a hundred years I could not forget that day, its festivities, those outbursts of joy by the people, delighted by the presence of their sovereign... What could equal those mythological figures? Those horses and chariots? Those sea-gods, coats of arms and glittering shields and in the middle of the River Ill whose flowing waters reflected, as from thousand mirrors, the brilliant emblems floating upon its surface? It was like the end of the world. All idea of time or place was lost. Nor were more substantial delights absent; oxen were roasted whole, wine flowed in abundance and so great was the quantity of bread that the poorest persons would leave it untouched upon the ground. In the evening the whole town was illuminated, the cathedral was one blaze of light from cross to foundation; every ornament of the building shone like a constellation of stars..."

Many years later Marie-Antoinette told Baroness Oberkirch:

"You come from a province, Baroness, that I found very beautiful and very loyal when I passed through it. I shall never forget that there I was first greeted by the French; it was there that they first called me their Queen."

Rococo *is an ornate style originating in France in the 18th century and approximately covering the Louis XV period. The word "rococo" is derived from the French* "rocaille"*, a word used to describe the rock and shell work of the Versailles grottoes.*

After the death of Louis XIV in 1715, a new artistic freedom emerged. A society focused on personal pleasure demanded variety, surprise and originality. French rococo interiors were designed as lively, total works of art in which architecture, relief sculpture and wall paintings were complemented by elegant furniture, enchanting small sculptures, ornamented mirror frames, delightful ceramics and silverware, a few easel paintings, and decorative tapestry.

Most rococo features are to be observed in the Rohan Palace apartments: continuous undulating curves, restless, fluid movement, imaginative treatment of natural forms, attenuated sprays and tendrils, floral garlands, animals, shells and leaves with formal scrolls, asymmetrical concave and convex forms creating sinuous lines.

THE ASSEMBLY HALL

Peter Paul Rubens (1577-1640) was a Flemish painter. He was a major proponent of the baroque style, which emphasized movement, colour and sensuousness. Rubens is well-known for his monumental altarpieces, his portraits, landscapes, and historical paintings of mythological and allegorical subjects.

The assembly hall is dominated by the huge tapestry relating the episode of the **Battle of the Milvian Bridge** between the Emperors Constantine and Maxentius. This battle was as fundamental to the Roman Empire as to christendom. **Rubens**' rendering of this tumultuous encounter draws on what might be termed cinematographic language. Maxentius' army tries to run away from Constantine's. The soldiers rush frantically over the bridge, but it collapses under their weight, and men and horses are sent plummeting into the river.

Constantine defeated his co-emperor Maxentius in 312 A.D. at the ***Battle of Milvian Bridge****, a bridge on the River Tiber some two miles upstream from central Rome. Later on Constantine also defeated his co-emperor Licinius, so that by 324 A.D. he had become the sole ruler of both the western and the eastern parts of the Roman Empire.*

The bulging eyes of the former and the dilated nostrils of the latter reflect the terror that grips them. Several hundred men died that day and Maxentius was one of them. On the tapestry he is shown with his head upside down, on the point of drowning in the river Tiber.

Europe

The stucco decoration of the assembly hall ceiling is as prolific as that of the king's bedchamber. The superb rococo cornices with waving outlines sending up foliage shoots towards the centre of the ceiling; the delicate birds with garlands of flowers in their tiny beaks; the vases filled with roses surrounded by acanthus leaves and scrolling tendrils; the sculptured cartouches in the corners of the ceiling devoted to the four parts of the world – these are some of the motifs that meet the upward gaze.

America

The four parts of the world: **Europe** carrying the royal attributes; **America** poised ready to shoot an arrow; Asia wearing a turban and Africa in feather headdress, holding a parasol as if to protect her lion.

The two console tables in carved gilt wood with ***brèche*** *violette* marble tops, as well as the big console table in richly carved gilt wood with its **onyx**-plated top, already belonged to this room in the 18th century. The two ***bergère*** armchairs perfectly match the decoration of the wooden panelling. They were acquired in 1999 and have thus been restored to their original place.

The four **cabriolet armchairs** (three from the Louis XV period, ca. 1740, and one copy) are covered with tapestries inspired by La Fontaine's Fables. A 19th century sofa in the same style completes the set. The Louis XV chandelier and the exuberant rococo decoration are endlessly reflected by the pier glasses facing each other.

A ***cabriolet armchair*** *has its armrests separated from the seat. The seat between the two arms is wide, enabling a lady to sit down wearing a large dress.*

Onyx, *a variety of chalcedony, is a semi-precious stone found in various regions of the world. It has been used for centuries in hard-stone carving and jewellery.*

Brèche *(Breccia) is a rock composed of broken fragments of minerals glued together with a fine-grained natural cement. The word has its origins in the Italian language, in which it means "stone made with cemented gravel".*

A **bergère** *is an upholstered low armchair with exposed wood frame and enclosed sides. The upholstered arms are shorter than the length of the seat, and a soft loose cushion rests on the seat base.*

The overdoors show scenes from the Old Testament.

Jacob asking for Rachel's hand.

Jacob fell in love with Rachel, the daughter of his uncle Laban. He approached Laban for permission to marry her. Laban agreed but stipulated a bride price, whereby Jacob was to work for him for seven years. After seven years he tricked Jacob into marrying Lea, the elder sister. When Jacob realised the deceit he was angry; however, the two men eventually came to an agreement. One week later, Jacob married Rachel too and worked for Laban for another seven years.

The ***flight of Lot.***

Lot, his wife and his daughters, are fleeing from Sodom, a city suffering divine punishment. Lot's wife looks back to see the destruction of Sodom and Gomorrah and turns immediately into a pillar of salt as punishment for disobeying the divine warning not to look back.

The ***dream of Pharaoh.***

Pharaoh dreamed that seven fat cattle came out of the river and fed on the grass. Whereupon seven lean cattle came out of the river and ate the seven fat cattle. Pharaoh had a second dream: seven fat ears of corn sprouted on one stalk, and then seven thin ears sprouted after them and swallowed the fat ears. Nobody else but Joseph was able to interpret the dream. Joseph told Pharaoh that the seven fat cattle and the seven fat ears symbolized seven years of plenty, while the seven lean cattle and the seven empty ears pointed to seven years of famine which would annihilate the abundance. Pharaoh was impressed, acknowledged Joseph's wisdom and put him in charge of the whole territory of Egypt.

The ***dream of Joseph.***

Joseph, Jacob's favourite son, was envied by his eleven half-brothers. When he was seventeen years old he had two dreams. In the first dream, all twelve of them were gathering wheat sheaves. Those gathered by his brothers bowed down to his own. In the second dream, the sun, the moon, and eleven stars bowed to Joseph himself. He reported these dreams to his brothers, who were very annoyed because the dreams implied the supremacy of Joseph over themselves. To get rid of him, they sold him to merchants carrying spices and perfumes across the desert to Egypt.

Powder-blue ground baluster-shaped vase

The panels above the mirrors between the windows are original works by Pierre-Ignace Parrocel. They represent The **Feeding of the Five Thousand** and **Jesus and the children**. In the corners of the room stand two large Chinese *famille rose* **Powder-blue ground baluster-shaped vases** (Qing dynasty, Qianlong period, ca. 1750-1780). The vases are placed on Louis XVI mahogany pedestals and are decorated with illustrations of the daily life of Chinese high-society ladies.

__Jesus and the children__ describes the following event : "Then were there brought unto him little children, that he should put his hands on them, and pray: and the disciples rebuked them. But Jesus said: Suffer the little children, and forbid them not, to come unto me: for of such is the kingdom of Heaven."

The __Feeding of the 5,000__ is also known as the "miracle of the five loaves and two fishes", because the Gospel of John reports that five barley loaves and two small fishes were used by Jesus to feed a multitude.

Two large *famille rose* vases from the same period, displaying bunches of flowers, dragonflies and butterflies on a light background, are no less remarkable.

Against the back wall of the room are placed two *famille verte* **fish bowls** (Qing dynasty, Kangxi period, 1662-1722), which were originally intended to grace the gardens and inner courtyards of houses.

These large Chinese porcelain __fish bowls__ have unusually elaborate and sculptural bronze mounts garnished with scrolls, curlicue acanthus leaves, claws and rams' heads. The finely worked legs are linked by a crossbar bearing at its centre a pine cone that echoes the urn above. (Louis XIV period, made in Europe)

THE LIBRARY

The library completes the *enfilade* of the king's apartments. This large space is adorned by paintings representing the four Evangelists: Saint Matthew with an angel, Saint Mark with a lion, Saint John with an eagle and Saint Luke with a bull.

Saint Matthew and Saint Mark flank the wide bay window overlooking the terrace. Saint John and Saint Luke are placed on either side of the door leading into the chapel.

Saint Matthew is a copy after **Pierre Mignard**; Saint John is a copy after **Charles Le Brun**; Saint Mark and Saint Luke are copies after **Charles de La Fosse**.

Saint John the Evangelist with an eagle

Pierre Mignard
(1612-1695)
was a French portrait painter and decorator. He spent twenty-two years in Italy and acquired a reputation which earned him a recall to Paris by the king. He painted ceilings at the Tuileries and Versailles and a great fresco composition for the dome of Val-de-Grâce, commissioned by the Queen Mother. After Le Brun's death Mignard was appointed painter in chief to Louis XIV.

Charles Le Brun
(1619-1690)
was a French painter and decorator. His emphatic, pompous talent was in keeping with the taste of the king, and thus he became a prominent figure in 17th century French art. He stamped his own personality on all that was produced in France during his lifetime. He was the originator of the Louis XIV style. The king declared him "the greatest French artist of all time".

Charles de La Fosse
(1636-1716)
was a French painter and decorator. He was a pupil of Le Brun. The dome of the Invalides in Paris is the only existing work which gives a full measure of his talent. His works and designs played a key role in the change from the French classical style which prevailed at Louis XIV's court to the lighter rococo style.

The central parts of the longitudinal walls are devoted to the royal portraits. On the west wall hangs the full-length portrait of **Louis XIV**, facing the portrait of Louis XV on the east wall.

The **fleur-de-lis** *is a stylized lily. It is specifically associated with the French monarchy in a historical context.*

Portrait of **Louis XIV** in coronation robes

This universally known full-length "official portrait" of Louis XIV was painted in 1701 by Hyacinthe Rigaud. The work had been commissioned by the king as a present to his grandson Philip V (1683 -1746), recently made King of Spain. However, Louis XIV became so infatuated with the painting that he had second thoughts and decided to keep it at Versailles. Today the original is in the Louvre. Many copies were made of this absolute image of royal power.

Louis XIV is shown standing, facing three-quarters left. The solemnity of the scene is enhanced by the heavy coronation robe embroidered with fleurs-de-lis.

A large marble pillar, decorated with relief depicting Justice, is seen to the right of the king.

Standing on a platform under a crimson canopy symbolizing power and wealth, the king is the very picture of majesty. A crown and a hand of justice rest on a stool covered with fleur-de-lis *drapery. The king holds the sceptre upside down and the sword of Charlemagne hangs at his left hip.*

Under the coronation robe gathered up on his shoulder, the monarch wears court dress: lace jabot and cuffs, red heeled shoes with diamond buckles, silk stockings held up by garters. On his chest he wears the collar of the Order of the Holy Spirit. A black wig conceals his baldness. His shapely legs, represented in the fourth position of classical ballet, look more like those of a young dancer than of a man 63 years old and suffering from gout.

The copy displayed in Strasbourg was painted by Pierre Mendan in the 1950s. It has replaced an 18th century copy destroyed during the French Revolution.

The portrait of Louis XV (1710-1774) in coronation robes is the last of the three successive portraits painted by Hyacinthe Rigaud: Louis XV at the ages of 5 (1715), 11 (1721) and 17 (1727). The royal function is glorified in the manner of the preceding reign. To allow the painter to work quietly in his studio, the king ordered the prior of the Royal Abbey of Saint-Denis to lend Rigaud the royal insignia – the symbols of royal power: crown, sceptre and hand of justice. All three portraits were much admired and many copies were commissioned. The current copy was painted in 1950 by A. Roger.

The tapestries

The remaining space in the upper part of the wall is devoted to four tapestries set into the white wooden panelling. They belong to the History of Constantine series, viz: The **Vision of the Emblem of Christ appearing to Constantine** and The **Baptism of Constantine**, on the east wall; **Constantine and Helena worshipping the True Cross** and The **Founding of Constantinople**, on the west wall. The tapestries hang in their original places.

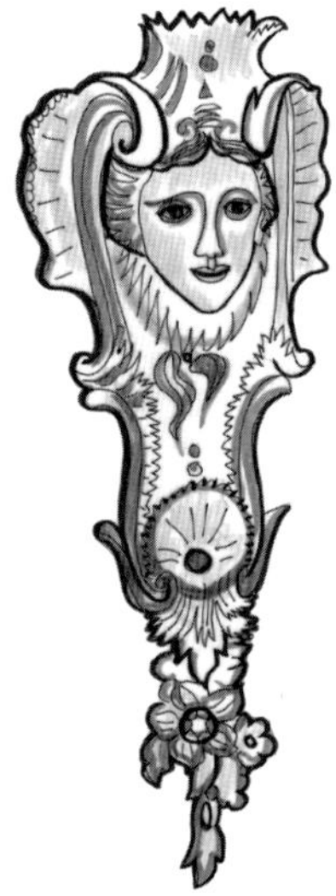

***Gilt-bronze** (ormolu) **mount** applied to the bookcases is made from bronze covered in ground gold mixed with mercury paste and heated. The technique is also known as "fire-gilding".*

The Founding of Constantinople

*In the year 330 A.D. **Constantine founded the city of Constantinople**. He transferred the imperial capital from Rome, its historic base, to Constantinople, henceforth officially called "the New Rome." After the fall of the West, Constantinople became the sole remaining capital of the Roman Empire and the largest and wealthiest city in Christendom between the fifth and the thirteenth centuries – a city radiating culture and learning.*

Constantine and Helena worshipping the True Cross

Legend has it that Constantine's mother, Saint Helena, travelled to the Holy Land in 326-28 A.D., founding churches and establishing charitable works for the poor. She discovered three crosses that were believed to have been used at the crucifixion of Jesus and the two thieves. A miracle revealed which of the three was the True Cross.

The Baptism of Constantine

Constantine is being baptized by Pope Sylvester in the Lateran baptistery in Rome. This image is not true to history. In 337 A.D., while in the eastern part of his empire, Constantine fell ill. He realized that he was dying and decided to be baptized. "The bishops performed the sacred ceremonies according to custom" and Constantine died in a royal villa in the vicinity of Nicomedia. He was buried in Constantinople.

The Vision of the Emblem of Christ appearing to Constantine

In this scene the chrism of Christ appears to Constantine in the sky at noon, some time before his encounter with Maxentius, his co-emperor. Later, Constantine had a dream in which Christ told him that by placing this emblem on his banner he would ensure victory over Maxentius: "In Hoc Signo Vinces" (under this sign you will conquer).

The seven bookcases made of solid mahogany, topped with Flemish marble and adorned with gilt-bronze mountings, originally contained some 3,400 books. These were dispersed and later replaced with 17th, 18th and 19th century books. The fireplace is made of the same marble as the shelves, and has the same shape, depth and height as the bookcases. All these elements make for a total visual unity. On top of the bookcases 37 copies of antique busts are displayed. Behind the bookcases, along the west wall, a tiny librarian's study is hidden.

***Mahogany** is a reddish-brown tropical hardwood prized for its beauty, durability and colour. It was first used by French cabinet-makers around 1720 and was widely used later during the Louis XVI and Empire periods.*

An impressive bust of Armand-Gaston de Rohan at the age of 56 has pride of place on the overmantel of the fireplace. The prince-bishop commissioned it from **Edmé Bouchardon** while staying in Rome in 1730 during the **Papal Conclave**. This work has a distinctly modern touch, in that the prince-bishop is depicted with real sincerity, both physically and psychologically.

Bust of Armand-Gaston de Rohan

In the 18th century the central part of the library was taken up by a large mahogany dining table matching the bookcases. It was later lost, but the tablecloth of Indo-Portuguese provenance reminds us of the size and the shape of the original table. The tablecloth is rarely exhibited, being valuable and fragile. It is embroidered with a profusion of conventionalized flowers and other Indian patterns influenced by Portuguese art. It bears witness to the long relationship between India and Portugal.

The terrestrial and celestial globes date from the 18th century.

There are two overdoors: "The Tribute Money", a painting after **Valentin de Boulogne**, illustrates the words of Jesus Christ: "Give therefore to Caesar the things that are Caesar's, and to God the things that are God's". The other one represents **Saint Catherine's Mystical Marriage**, after **Alessandro Turchi**, known as Alessandro Veronese. The original paintings belonged to Louis XIV.

Saint Catherine's Mystical Marriage

Edmé Bouchardon *(1698-1762) was a celebrated French sculptor and draughtsman. At the age of 25 he left for Rome, where he executed the bust of Pope Clement XIII. Back in France, he became sculptor to the king in 1732 and in 1746 he produced his masterpiece "Cupid Fashioning a Bow out of Hercules' Club", now in the Louvre Museum.*

*A **Papal Conclave** is a meeting of the College of Cardinals convened to elect the Pope. The conclave has been the procedure for choosing the Pope for almost a thousand years. During the vote the cardinals are locked in the Sistine Chapel in the Apostolic Palace. Armand-Gaston, a cardinal since 1712, attended four conclaves. On each occasion he took advantage of his stay in Rome to buy works of art or have copies made.*

Valentin de Boulogne *(1591-1632) was a French painter who spent the major part of his life in Rome. He was influenced by Caravaggio's naturalistic style and his way of rendering contrasts between light and dark. Valentin had success with a type of composition invented by Caravaggio, in which fortune tellers, drinkers, gamblers or musicians are grouped around a table.*

***Alessandro Turchi**, called Alessandro Veronese (1578-1649), was an Italian painter of the early Baroque, born and mainly active in Verona. In 1638 he joined the papal guild of artists and moved to Rome.*

THE CHAPEL

The chapel is entered through a large door covered with mirrors. There is no wooden panelling here and few rococo shapes. The Versailles parquet floor has given way to octagons of Comblanchien limestone with cabochons in black marble. At first sight the walls seem to be covered with a selection of colourful marbles. However, they are actually covered with a perfect marble imitation called **scagliola**.

The northern wall of the chapel looks very solemn with its four bluish pilasters topped with gilded Corinthian capitals. The pilasters form a frame which sets off the painting hung in the middle of the wall, called the **Adoration of the Shepherds**. It is a copy after the original by Corregio painted in 1530, and is also called

Scagliola *is a composite substance made from selenite, glue and natural pigments, imitating costly marbles and other hard stones. It is polished with linseed oil for brightness, and waxed for protection. The combination of materials permits a variety of colours not available in natural veined marbles. Scagliola can be used to produce stucco columns, sculptures, and other architectural elements.*

Antonio Allegri da ***Correggio*** *(ca.1489-1534) was the foremost painter of the Parma school of the Italian Renaissance. He painted some of the most vigorous and sensuous works of the 16th century. He used dynamic composition, illusionist perspective and dramatic foreshortening. He is considered as a forerunner of chiaroscuro. He decorated the dome of Parma cathedral with a startling Assumption of the Virgin, crowded with a vortex of receding figures.*

"The Night". The artist has achieved an outstanding result in his treatment of light, which seems to gush out of the body of the newborn Jesus and flood the Virgin Mary and the group of shepherds. One of the women present in the stable moves back in awe, shading her eyes with her hand from the intense, uncanny light. The upper left corner features a cluster of angels.

The Adoration of the Shepherds *(detail); this painting is now housed in the Old Masters Picture Gallery in Dresden, Germany.*

Paul Ponce Antoine Robert, known as ***Robert de Séry*** *(1686-1733), was a French painter who spent many years in Italy. He was commissioned by Armand-Gaston de Rohan, whom he followed to Paris in 1725. He established his studio in the magnificent palace which his patron owned in Paris, at 87 rue Vieille du Temple, today host to the "Archives nationales".*

To the left side on the same wall is another copy after Corregio: The **Virgin Mary with Child, Saint Jerome, Mary-Magdalene and John the Baptist**. In this painting the expression of the Virgin is pure gentleness. The Christ-child is very much alive; he reaches for the book presented by an angel, while at the same time he is stroking Mary-Magdalene's hair. The latter, moved by his presence, touches his foot tenderly. Saint Jerome is escorted by his lion.

On the right side of the wall hangs a copy painted after the Madonna della Scodella (Virgin with a bowl), also known as The **Rest on the Flight to Egypt**, by Antonio da Correggio. In this scene of family happiness, the Virgin half smiles at the Christ-child, who holds his parents' hands. Joseph's face radiates felicity.

The three copies in the chapel were painted by **Robert de Séry**, who was "painter in ordinary to the prince-bishop". Robert went to Modena and Parma, where the originals happened to be at that time.

Virgin with Child, Saint Jerome, Saint Mary-Magdalene and Saint John the Baptist and Virgin with a bowl

A huge carpet covers most of the floor. It was woven "in the Turkish fashion" in 1745 at the **Aubusson** tapestry works and testifies to the taste for comfort and luxury of the first prince-bishop and cardinal. The centre of the carpet features his coat of arms, surmounted by the cardinal's hat.

We leave the chapel through a small, unobtrusive door, walking past the private staircase and into the prince-bishop's private apartments, which run parallel to the king's. The first room on our way is the dressing-room; we then proceed through the study, the bedchamber and the antechamber, eventually leaving the private apartments for the synod hall, where we began our visit.

***Aubusson** is a town in the Creuse, a rural region of central France. Aubusson is well known for its tapestry and carpets, which have been famous world-wide since the 14th century, when Flemish weavers came to live here. In the 17th century, the Aubusson workshops were given "royal warrant" status by Jean-Baptiste Colbert, Louis XIV's minister of finance.*

Private staircase

THE DRESSING-ROOM

The ***Manufacture nationale de Sèvres*** *was founded in 1740 with the support of Louis XV and Madame de Pompadour and was first located in Vincennes. In 1756 the factory moved to Sèvres, near Madame de Pompadour's château. Initially it produced a soft-paste porcelain, until the first kaolin deposit on French soil was discovered near Limoges in 1768. Two years later, hard-paste porcelain began to be manufactured and marketed in Sèvres.*

The overdoors are originals by Pierre-Ignace Parrocel representing Canon Law and Magnanimity. In the showcase are displayed **Sèvres** porcelain armorial dessert pieces, commissioned by Louis-René de Rohan in 1772 before he left for Vienna (Austria) to take up his post as French ambassador.

Plate with Louis-René de Rohan's monogram

Through a glass door in the corner of the dressing-room we can peep into the "water closet". This is one of the very few amenities of its kind to have survived until the present day, even though in this case the close stool (commode chair) has disappeared and the original bidet has been replaced by a copy. In the water closet, a mirror reflects a painting by Pierre-Ignace Parrocel, in which a group of cherubs play around a **sleeping Eros**. One of the little rascals is about to administer him a clyster (enema), while another one urinates in his quiver.

*Andiron **guard** with mythological figures*

The fireplace is equipped with an exceptional pair of **andirons**, with **guards** elaborately ornamented in Louis XV style, and a **fireback** with a coat of arms. On either side of the fireplace stand two Louis XV walnut chairs.

*An **andiron** is a horizontal iron bar upon which logs are laid for burning. Andirons are used in pairs to form a firedog supporting the logs in order to improve air circulation for better combustion. They usually stand on short legs with an upright guard to keep the logs in the fireplace.*

*A **fireback** is a piece of heavy cast iron placed against the back wall of the fireplace. Its function is to protect the wall behind, and to store heat and radiate it into the room. It makes for a more efficient fire.*

Sleeping Eros

THE PRINCE-BISHOP'S STUDY

History

In this brightly lit room the corners of the ceiling feature four allegories: **History**, Philosophy, Astronomy and Fine Arts. During the Napoleonic period the study was refurnished to become the emperor's bedroom.

The sofa, armchairs and chairs were made for empress Josephine in 1807. The emperor's bed dates from the same period. The upholstery fabric is modern but imitates the original pattern. The Empire-style circular mahogany pedestal table with lion claw legs and eagle heads dates from 1805.

The overdoors represent The Holy Family and The **Arcadian Shepherds**, after **Nicolas Poussin**. The painting above the mirror between the windows is a copy of **Erminia and Tancred**, after **Pier Francesco Mola.**

Arcadian shepherds

On the pedestal table is a large **lidded jar** (Japan, 17th century). On the fireplace overmantel are displayed bottle-shaped *famille rose* graviata vases (Qing dynasty, Qianlong period 1736-1795) with tiny in-the-round figures of creeping **dragons**.

Lidded jar

The painting ***Erminia and Tancred*** *is about an impossible love between two characters torn between feelings and duty. It was inspired by "Jerusalem delivered", a poem by Torquato Tasso (1544-1595).*

The name Arcadia, a region of the Peloponnese in Greece, has become a poetic byword for a mythical unspoiled wilderness, where shepherds live in harmony with nature. In Poussin's painting the ***Arcadian shepherds*** *discover a gravestone, which makes them realise that death exists even in the idyllic land of Arcadia.*

Nicolas Poussin *(Andelys 1594-Rome 1665) was a French classical painter who spent the major part of his working life in Rome. Most of his works treat religious or mythological subjects, with an important landscape element thrown in. His painting is characterized by clarity, logic and order. He favoured line over colour.*

Pier Francesco Mola*, (1612 Ticino, today a Swiss canton-1666) was an Italian painter of the High Baroque, working mainly in Rome. He was interested in exploring landscape elements.*

Dragons are emblematic of imperial power in China

THE PRINCE-BISHOP'S CHAMBER

Torchere

The chamber contains a series of pieces dating from the time when the palace was refurnished by Napoleon: a 1770 sofa with a triangular seat at each end, called *canapé à confidents*; six armchairs, six upright chairs and a fire screen. Two small Japanese black and gilt-lacquered cabinets date from the end of the 17th century. Two Louis XVI **torcheres** (candlestands) come from the palace in Saverne. The Louis XVI roll-top desk is equipped with a revolving cylinder that locks down to hide confidential papers when the desk is not in use. On top of the desk stands a biscuit-ware vase which Joseph Hannong presented to Louis XVI and Marie-Antoinette in 1781, hoping that the royal couple would help him to resolve his financial problems. All in vain… The pedal harp was made in 1782 in Strasbourg by R. Storck.

The rear wall is hung with crimson damask. In the middle hangs a tapestried door curtain with the prince-bishop's coat of arms. This tapestry, which was woven around 1725, used to hang in front of a door to keep out draughts. There are also four paintings – from left to right: a portrait of Comte de Ruet by **Alexis Simon Belle**; The **Death of Cleopatra** and The **Death of Lucretia** by François de Troy; The **deification of Aeneas** by **Jean II Restout**.

The overdoors are modern copies of 18th century copies after **Annibale Carracci**, dedicated to Hunting and Fishing. The 18th century copies were destroyed during the bombing in 1944.

Biscuit-ware vase manufactured by Joseph Hannong

Annibale Carracci *(Bologna 1560-1609) was the author of masterly frescoes and drawings. He played a significant part in the evolution of Italian painting in the 17th century.*

Concerning the ***Suicide of Cleopatra*** *(69 B.C.-30 B.C.), Plutarch reports that an asp was concealed in a basket of figs that was brought to her. She found it and let it bite her. Cleopatra is frequently depicted with an asp at her breast.*

*The **deification of Aeneas** was inspired by Virgil's Aeneid. In Greek mythology, Aeneas is a Trojan hero, the son of Prince Anchises and the goddess Aphrodite. Virgil described him as an ancestor of Romulus and Remus and the first true hero of Rome.*

***Lucretia** was a legendary Roman noblewoman whose fate greatly influenced the History of Rome. She stabbed herself to death around 509 B.C. after being raped by the son of King Lucius Tarquinius Superbus. Her violent death was the immediate cause of a rebellion that overthrew the monarchy and instituted the republic.*

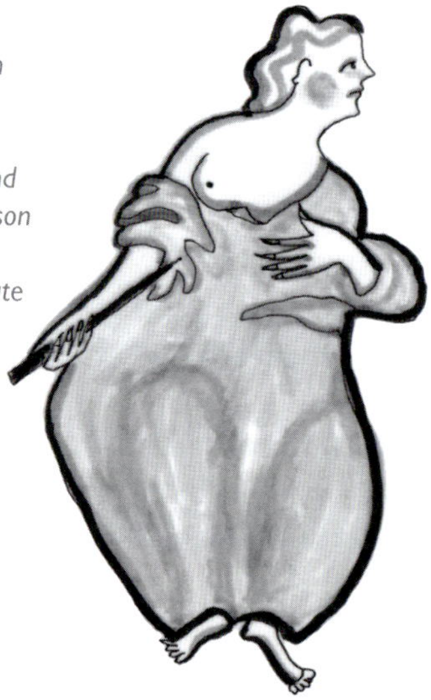

Jean-François de Troy
(Paris 1679-Rome 1752) was a French rococo painter and tapestry designer. His art – whether history, portraits, genre or decorative – was much admired. It gives a number of clues to contemporary manners, fashions and pastimes.

Jean II Restout
(Rouen1692-1768) was a French rococo painter whose altar-pieces, ceilings and designs for Gobelin tapestries were highly valued.

Alexis-Simon Belle
(1674-1734) was a French portrait painter of the French and Jacobite nobility.

THE PRINCE-BISHOP'S ANTECHAMBER

Carlo Maratta *(1625-1713) was an Italian painter, chiefly known for his classicizing paintings.*

Antoine Coypel *(1661-1722) was a French historical painter. His most accomplished work was the decoration of the ceiling of the Royal chapel at Versailles in the Roman baroque manner.*

Alexandre-François Desportes *(1661-1743) was a French painter and decorative designer specialising in animals. Louis XIV and Louis XV commissioned from him portraits of their favourite hounds. In several paintings he combined game with a buffet of spectacular pieces in silver, thus documenting the lost silverware of Louis XIV.*

The antechamber suffered damage during the American bombings of 1944 and was therefore partly rebuilt. Originally the overdoors were painted after the masterpieces of Versailles, viz: the Preaching of Saint John the Baptist and the Nativity, by **Carlo Maratta**; Moses defends the daughters of Jethro, and Moses marries Zipporah, by Charles Le Brun; Rebecca and Eliezer, by **Antoine Coypel**; the Finding of Moses, by Charles de La Fosse. After their disappearance in the bombing, these old copies were partly replaced by modern ones.

The large decorative composition is a 1727 work by **Alexandre-François Desportes**.

The tiled stove was manufactured in Strasbourg in the 18th century by Acker. It comes from the *Jardin d'Angleterre* mansion at *La Wantzenau*. Its shape echoes that of the stove originally present in this room.

Tiled stove

The two **pagodas** in white and blue porcelain (Qing dynasty, Qianlong period, 1736-1795) are fine specimens from Louis-René de Rohan's Chinese collection. They are 155 cm (61 inches) high and recall a 79 m (260 feet) high porcelain tower in Nanjing, built in the 15th century during the Ming dynasty. There are also two large cylindrical vases (Qing dynasty, Qianlong period 1736-1795).

Pagoda (detail)

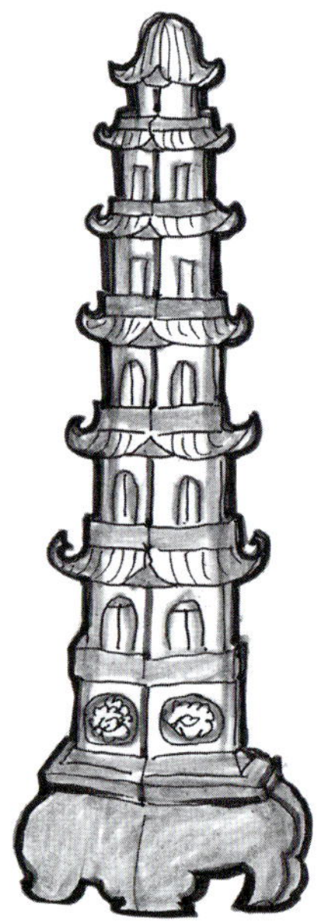

Pagoda

This very rare ebony and ormolu cabinet on its own stand was made around 1675 in a Parisian workshop working for the Crown. It is supported by gilded caryatids representing the four seasons. The architecture of the front is enhanced by the pilasters. The drawers are arranged on either side of a central niche framed by two gilded columns. The front displays images of perching birds, flowers, floral sprays and a central flower-filled vase. The images rely on an inlay technique called "*pietra dura*", using highly polished coloured stones such as lapis lazuli and porphyry precisely cut and fitted together. Strong colours seek to achieve a contrast with the ebony.

COLLECTIONS OF THE MUSEUM OF DECORATIVE ARTS

FAIENCE

(GLAZED EARTHENWARE)

To round off our tour of the apartments, and for a better acquaintance with the way of life in 18th century Strasbourg, why not visit the former stables, now converted into a museum of decorative arts ?

After belonging to the Holy Roman Empire of the German Nation for centuries, Strasbourg was incorporated into the Kingdom of France by Louis XIV in 1681 and granted the status of "free royal city", whereupon many prominent persons from the highest echelons of the French nobility, as well as francophile German princely families, poured into the town. These great aristocrats sought a way of life appropriate to their position. The palaces they built were stamped with the influence of Versailles, and their new homes were filled with furniture, manufactured articles and valuable things in keeping with the latest fashion.

The bourgeoisie of Strasbourg kept a close watch on all these developments, which inspired them to change their surroundings. In their new houses, behind the stonework façades "*à la française*" sporting French balconies and mascarons, the walls of their apartments came to be covered with wooden panelling painted in pale colours; their new furniture acquired undulating curves; upholstered armchairs ousted wooden chairs; stylish parquet replaced simple wooden flooring; fireplaces drove out stoves; stucco decorations, friezes, cornices and rosettes invaded the ceilings.

Trompe-l'œil *glazed earthenware tureen in the shape of a turkey, Hannong (1754-1760)*

The young ladies of Strasbourg became disdainful of the pewterware so admired by their mothers, and instead acquired **faience** – a fine, floral earthenware – produced by the Hannong factory. In the course of six decades (1721-1781) the rise and fall of Strasbourg

THE LARGE CENTRAL ROOM

The large central room is impressive with its two main showcases emphasizing poultry and game, but also vegetables and fruit. The naturalist forms served as *pâté* or soup tureens. This type of piece, dating from the period 1754-1760, earned the factory the favours of a princely clientele.

In the middle of the room, "*trompe-l'œil*" delicacies are set out on a table to tempt imaginary guests – hard-boiled eggs, olives, artichokes etc. The smaller showcases contain little faience characters disguised as hunters, shepherds and shepherdesses, in settings derived from Meissen porcelain groups.

Duck-shaped tureen,
Paul Hannong,
ca. 1745-1762

Pigeon-shaped tureen,
Paul Hannong,
ca. 1745-1762

Capercaillie-shaped tureen,
Pierre Hannong
(a son of Paul Hannong),
Haguenau,
ca. 1761-1762

Cabbage-shaped tureen,
Hannong (1748-1754)

"Compotier" *(fruit bowl) with green olives, Hannong (1745-1754)*

Square "hors-d'œuvres" *dish with quarters of hard-boiled eggs, Hannong (1745-1754)*

THE BLUE ROOM

The blue room contains beautiful dishes and plates of the period 1748-1760, when production was in full swing. The "***fleurs fines***" (rimless flowers) seen here have been produced either with a **pouncing pattern** or a **template**. They may also have been inspired by engravings or natural flowers.

Showcase No 1: Flowers painted with the template technique

Showcase No 2: "*Fleurs fines*" ; decoration thought to have been painted by Christian Wilhelm von Löwenfinck, his wife Maria Serapha, or their pupils.

Showcase No 3: "*Fleurs fines*" produced with a pouncing pattern.

Showcase No 4: "*Fleurs fines*" produced without either pouncing pattern or template.

Showcase No 5: Three pieces decorated with "*fleurs fines*"and blue and gilt highlights.

Pouncing pattern *– Pounce is a fine powder, usually charcoal, that is tapped through perforations in paper corresponding to the main lines of a design, in order to transfer it to another surface.*

Template *is a simple way to reproduce shapes – e.g. concentric circles forming a rose.*

Fleurs fines, *as opposed to* "fleurs chatironnées", *are not outlined by a thin black line.*

Oval dish, "fleurs fines", *Paul Hannong, Strasbourg or Haguenau (1754-1762)*

COLLECTIONS OF THE MUSEUM OF DECORATIVE ARTS

FAIENCE

(GLAZED EARTHENWARE)

To round off our tour of the apartments, and for a better acquaintance with the way of life in 18th century Strasbourg, why not visit the former stables, now converted into a museum of decorative arts ?

After belonging to the Holy Roman Empire of the German Nation for centuries, Strasbourg was incorporated into the Kingdom of France by Louis XIV in 1681 and granted the status of "free royal city", whereupon many prominent persons from the highest echelons of the French nobility, as well as francophile German princely families, poured into the town. These great aristocrats sought a way of life appropriate to their position. The palaces they built were stamped with the influence of Versailles, and their new homes were filled with furniture, manufactured articles and valuable things in keeping with the latest fashion.

The bourgeoisie of Strasbourg kept a close watch on all these developments, which inspired them to change their surroundings. In their new houses, behind the stonework façades "*à la française*" sporting French balconies and mascarons, the walls of their apartments came to be covered with wooden panelling painted in pale colours; their new furniture acquired undulating curves; upholstered armchairs ousted wooden chairs; stylish parquet replaced simple wooden flooring; fireplaces drove out stoves; stucco decorations, friezes, cornices and rosettes invaded the ceilings.

Trompe-l'œil *glazed earthenware tureen in the shape of a turkey, Hannong (1754-1760)*

The young ladies of Strasbourg became disdainful of the pewterware so admired by their mothers, and instead acquired **faience** – a fine, floral earthenware – produced by the Hannong factory. In the course of six decades (1721-1781) the rise and fall of Strasbourg faience manufacture was complete; it went through a promising initial stage, a period of international fame, then a drastic collapse followed by a sudden shutdown in production.

Faience is a soft-paste, delicate, pale type of earthenware made from damp clay mixed with other materials. Preparing the ceramic paste involves a number of operations – extracting the clay, crushing it, mixing it with water and letting it settle, straining it through a sieve and making the final mixture, called the clay body, which will incorporate some other ingredients such as calcareous marl or feldspar. The clay body must then be stored and aged in a cellar. In due course it will be moulded, modelled or shaped on a potter's wheel. After a lengthy drying process, the final pieces are fired in a kiln at a temperature of 900 °C (1652 °F). Firing hardens the clay. Following this initial "mild firing", the pieces are glazed and paint is applied on the raw glaze. They then go through a second firing, at 1100 °C (2012 °F). The fired glaze makes the surface of the pottery shiny, decorative and waterproof. The decoration obtained in this way is called "*grand feu*" decoration. Unlike porcelain, faience is not translucent.

In Italy, the town of Faenza was renowned for the beauty and quality of its glazed earthenware pottery which, from the Renaissance onwards, was exported to different countries. The word "**faience**"*, which refers to this type of ceramics, is derived from the name of the town.*

Petit feu *is a technique whereby a motif is applied to an already glazed and fired ceramic object. It is subsequently fired at a lower temperature (600-800 °C) (1112 °F-1472 °F) in a special "muffle kiln". This technique offers a richer colour range, because many more colours can withstand the second firing at a lower temperature.*

Over six decades, three generations of Hannongs created innovative styles and techniques, raising earthenware to new levels of sophistication and refinement. The firing procedure at lower temperatures, referred to as "***petit feu***", makes it possible to use a wider range of colours, including different shades of red, colours that had not been able to survive the traditional "*grand-feu*" firing temperature. Thanks to the "*petit feu*" technique, the Hannongs excelled in naturalistic flower patterns and bouquets incorporating gracefully sweeping stems, applied to plates, dishes and tureens. Strasbourg faience products include large tureens designed by Paul Hannong, in such shapes as pumpkins, cabbages, cauliflowers as well as animal figures – wild boars, ducks, geese, pigeons or turkeys.

Oval dish, ca. 1735/1740-1754, mixed technique, Paul or Balthazar Hannong

Charles-François Hannong (Maastricht ca. 1669-Strasbourg (?) 1739) was the founder of the Hannong faience dynasty. In 1709 this Dutch pipe maker settled in Strasbourg, where he set up a faience factory in 1721. A few years later he founded a second factory in **Haguenau**, a place where firewood and quality clay were plentiful.

In 1730, when Charles-François retired, the Strasbourg factory fell to **Paul Hannong** (1700-1760), while Balthazar Hannong (1703-1753) took charge of Haguenau. A few years later Paul Hannong assumed control of both establishments and became the sole master of the family business. In the period between 1745 and 1748, Paul introduced the "*petit feu*" technique and managed to persuade a number of exceptionally skilful painters to leave Meissen for Strasbourg. Among these were Christian Wilhelm von Löwenfinck (1720-1753), soon followed by his brother, Adam Friedrich von Löwenfinck (1714-1754), who was in charge of production from 1748 to his death, when his wife Maria Serapha took over. Then Joseph Jacob Ringler (1730-1804), a painter and chemist who had been trained in porcelain manufacture in Vienna, followed suit – and revealed to Paul Hannong the trade secret of **Cassius purple**.

Haguenau *is a town some 30 km (19 miles) to the north of Strasbourg. It lies south of the forest of Haguenau, the biggest forest in Alsace and one of the largest in France (some 51,000 acres).*

Paul Hannong longed to produce porcelain. He succeeded in 1751, probably thanks to the advice of Joseph Jacob Ringler. When, in 1753, the French authorities granted the "*Manufacture de Sèvres*" the exclusive right to produce porcelain in France, Paul Hannong had to transfer his business to Frankenthal in Germany. The production of hard paste porcelain in Frankenthal turned out to be successful, but Paul died in 1760.

Joseph Hannong (1734-after 1800), his son, ran the family business from 1762 to 1780. Joseph sold the Frankenthal factory with a view to producing porcelain in Strasbourg with the help and under the protection of prince-bishop Louis-César-Constantin de Rohan (1697-1779), from whom he borrowed huge amounts of money. After the bishop's death, Joseph was summoned to honour his debts, but since that was beyond him, he was declared bankrupt in 1780.

Cassius purple *is a purple pigment formed by the reaction of gold salts with stannous chloride ($SnCl^2$).*

THE PINK ROOM

The pieces shown in the pink room were manufactured by Charles-François. These white exhibits are decorated with blue patterns applied using the "*grand feu*" technique. The braid and valance (embroidered style) decoration was influenced by the **Rouen factory**, an important pottery production centre at the time.

Helmet-shaped ewer, Charles-François, Paul or Balthazar Hannong, Strasbourg, 1725-1754

Showcase No. 1

The pieces of this period – table centrepieces, tureens and stands, "*pots à oille*" (soup tureens), saucers, basins, bowls, table fountains, wine coolers, ewers, jugs and plates – have simple but varied shapes – circular, oval, octagonal, rectangular or square with cut corners.

Showcase No. 2

The pieces in this showcase reflect the evolution of shapes and profiles pursued by Paul Hannong from the beginning of the 1730s: helmet-shaped ewers; pyramidal table centrepieces with dolphins and human masks; diamond-shaped tureens with rounded corners. The lines softened; flowers and fruit became more natural.

Showcase No. 3

In this showcase the green artichoke-shaped knob on a tureen lid is the first example of an attempt at colour diversification.

*The **Rouen factory** (Normandy) began producing fine earthenware in the 16th century and soft-paste porcelain in the 17th century. Both were much appreciated by French aristocrats.*

Oval dish, ca. 1735/1740-1754, mixed technique decoration, Paul or Balthazar Hannong

THE GREEN ROOM

Tray with "Indian flower" decoration, mixed technique, Paul or Balthazar Hannong, Strasbourg, ca. 1735-1748

Melon-shaped tureen, mixed technique, Paul Hannong, ca. 1745-1748

Baroque tureen with sculptural lid knob, mixed technique, Paul or Balthazar Hannong, Strasbourg, ca. 1745-1748

The showcases in the green room display a greater number of multi-coloured items.

Showcase No. 1

Here we see products from the years 1745-1748, with decoration inspired by the Far East: covered soup bowls, sugar bowls and a **tray** with an imaginary oriental scene.

Showcase No. 2

is inhabited by little Chinese characters and by exotic animals transformed into perfume-burners. A naturalistic **melon-shaped tureen** and a **baroque tureen** with a wavy, scalloped rim, inspired by the stucco decoration of the Rohan Palace apartments, are indicative of the aesthetic directions followed by the Hannong factory.

Showcases No. 3 and No. 4

display plates decorated with "Indian flowers" from the period 1730-1735. The loosely scattered flowers point to a Hannong predilection for floral ornamentation. The flowers are stylised and "*chatironnées*", which means that they are outlined by a thin black line.

THE LARGE CENTRAL ROOM

The large central room is impressive with its two main showcases emphasizing poultry and game, but also vegetables and fruit. The naturalist forms served as *pâté* or soup tureens. This type of piece, dating from the period 1754-1760, earned the factory the favours of a princely clientele.

In the middle of the room, "*trompe-l'œil*" delicacies are set out on a table to tempt imaginary guests – hard-boiled eggs, olives, artichokes etc. The smaller showcases contain little faience characters disguised as hunters, shepherds and shepherdesses, in settings derived from Meissen porcelain groups.

Duck-shaped tureen,
Paul Hannong,
ca. 1745-1762

Pigeon-shaped tureen,
Paul Hannong,
ca. 1745-1762

Capercaillie-shaped tureen,
Pierre Hannong
(a son of Paul Hannong),
Haguenau,
ca. 1761-1762

Cabbage-shaped tureen, Hannong (1748-1754)

"Compotier" *(fruit bowl) with green olives, Hannong (1745-1754)*

Square "hors-d'œuvres" *dish with quarters of hard-boiled eggs, Hannong (1745-1754)*

THE BLUE ROOM

The blue room contains beautiful dishes and plates of the period 1748-1760, when production was in full swing. The "***fleurs fines***" (rimless flowers) seen here have been produced either with a **pouncing pattern** or a **template**. They may also have been inspired by engravings or natural flowers.

Showcase No 1: Flowers painted with the template technique

Showcase No 2: "*Fleurs fines*" ; decoration thought to have been painted by Christian Wilhelm von Löwenfinck, his wife Maria Serapha, or their pupils.

Showcase No 3: "*Fleurs fines*" produced with a pouncing pattern.

Showcase No 4: "*Fleurs fines*" produced without either pouncing pattern or template.

Showcase No 5: Three pieces decorated with "*fleurs fines*"and blue and gilt highlights.

Pouncing pattern *– Pounce is a fine powder, usually charcoal, that is tapped through perforations in paper corresponding to the main lines of a design, in order to transfer it to another surface.*

Template *is a simple way to reproduce shapes – e.g. concentric circles forming a rose.*

Fleurs fines, *as opposed to "fleurs chatironnées", are not outlined by a thin black line.*

Oval dish, "fleurs fines", Paul Hannong, Strasbourg or Haguenau (1754-1762)

Round plate, "fleurs fines",
Paul Hannong (1748-1754)

Round plate, "fleurs fines",
with blue and gilt highlights

Round plate, "fleurs fines",
Paul Hannong (1745-1754)

Round plate, "fleurs fines",
Paul Hannong, Strasbourg or
Haguenau (1754-1762)

GOLDSMITHERY

The 18th century was the golden age (no pun intended!) for Strasbourg's goldsmiths. They were renowned for the outstanding quality of their **vermeil** (silver-gilt). When Strasbourg became a French royal city in 1681, the city goldsmiths gained from their contact with fashionable Parisian circles. The city's geographical situation, straddling the German and French worlds, enabled them to provide luxury products to the francophile German princely courts, where "*la mode française*" was much appreciated.

The local presence of members of the French nobility such as the prince-bishop and cardinal, the representative of the King of France, the military governor, etc. generated an important demand for costly items. Well-off protestants ordered hymn books with gilded bindings, while the catholic priests reinstated in the city churches were seeking vermeil cult objects. As to middle-class households, they were keen to follow the latest fashions and would purchase vermeil teapots, coffeepots, hot chocolate pots, sugar bowls, beakers and mustard pots.

It was not easy to become a master goldsmith. A candidate served a four-year apprenticeship, after which he became a journeyman and embarked on his "*compagnonnage*" (an eight-year working trip). In order to be recognized as a master, the journeyman had to submit a "masterpiece" as proof of his skills. Validation of the masterpiece by the guild and the passing of a final examination were conditions for obtaining master status.

***Vermeil** is gilded silver. Vermeil pieces bear a visual similarity to gold, but are much cheaper and lighter than solid gold. They are used for table plate, toiletry sets and grand decorative pieces. The original fire-gilding process was developed in France in the mid-18th century; however, France later banned the production of vermeil because over time artisans became blind due to the mercury used in the process. Today, vermeil is safely produced by electrolysis. It does not blacken or cause allergies.*

***Morocco leather** is a kind of soft leather traditionally associated with bookbinding, wallets, lining for fine luggage and the like. The finest grades of morocco leather are goatskin.*

*A set of six silver-gilt coffee spoons by Johann Remichius Berentz and Johann Jacob Hauser (second quarter of the 18th century), original case of tawny **morocco leather** with red buckskin*

The goldsmiths' shops were often located in the present *Rue des Orfèvres*. Goldsmiths used to constitute real dynasties, such as the Imlins or the Kirsteins.

During the 18th century the number of Strasbourg goldsmiths grew steadily. On the eve of the French Revolution there were a hundred of them. As might be expected, the revolutionary years dealt a fatal blow to the profession; not only was it almost wiped out, but a great part of the existing gold and silverware was melted down in order to recover the precious metals. The objects included in the Strasbourg collection are miraculous survivals of the way of life "*à la française*" through the "***Ancien Régime***" period.

Hymnal bound with silver-gilt and crimson silk velvet, Isaac Kubler

*The "**Ancien Régime**" was the social and political system that prevailed in the Kingdom of France before it was overthrown by the French Revolution in 1789.*

Silver-gilt écuelle (soup tureen) with cover and stand (1767), handles chased with scrolls, by Johann Ludwig (III) Imlin

The rather simple shape of this tureen is enhanced by its exuberant floral decoration – roses, lilies, bellflowers, sunflowers, daisies, peonies and, last but not least, the artichoke-shaped lid knob resting on acanthus leaves.

Mirror, mirror on the wall, tell me a story about a prince charming and a beautiful princess...

Once upon a time, there lived in the city of Strasbourg a prince called **Maximilien-Joseph de Deux-Ponts** (Zweibrücken) (1756-1825), of the house of Wittelsbach. In 1786 he presented this magnificent mirror to his young wife **Augusta-Wilhelmine of Hesse-Darmstadt** (1765-1796), who had borne him a son.

The baby, called **Louis** (Ludwig), was godson and namesake of King Louis XVI of France. At the time of his birth, his father was an officer in the French army stationed at Strasbourg and he lived with his family in the present *Palais du Gouverneur*, between *13, Rue Brûlée* and *Place Broglie*.

The French Revolution drove Maximilien and his family out of Strasbourg. They spent a few years in Mannheim in rather modest circumstances. Four more children were born to the couple; unfortunately, Augusta Wilhelmine died from exhaustion and tuberculosis in a castle near Heidelberg.

Maximilien remarried, and his second wife Caroline of Baden (1776-1841) thus became the owner of the famous mirror. She bore eight children, of whom five daughters survived. One of them was later to be the mother of Franz Joseph (Emperor of Austria), and another one would become the mother of Sissi (Elisabeth of Austria).

Maximilien's hereditary lands were invaded by Napoleon's army. Max, reasonably enough, chose to support Napoleon. He gave his daughter **Augusta-Amélie** (Augusta Amalia) in marriage to **Eugène de Beauharnais**, Napoleon's adoptive son. From Maximilien's hereditary possessions the Emperor of the French created the Kingdom of Bavaria, with Max as its first king.

In 1813 **King Maximilien** changed sides, joined the Allies against Napoleon and formally declared war on France, in return for which the Allies undertook to guarantee the integrity of his Bavarian kingdom. After his death his son, whose birth had led to the making of the mirror, became in turn King of Bavaria under the name **Ludwig I of Bavaria**.

What about the mirror? Well, the complex rules of inheritance caused it to end up in Vienna, where it fell to the Red Army as its share of booty at the end of the 2nd World War. In 1953 it turned up at an auction in Bern (Switzerland), where it was acquired for the Museum of Decorative Arts in Strasbourg.

Augusta Amalia Ludovika of Bavaria *(Strasbourg 1788-Munich 1851) married* ***Eugène de Beauharnais*** *(1781-1824), the son of Josephine de Beauharnais. Although savouring of a political alliance, this marriage turned out to be a happy one. Augusta and Eugène had seven children.*

Ludwig *(Strasbourg 1786-Nice 1868),* ***King of Bavaria*** *(1825-1848), succeeded his father on the throne in 1825. Ludwig transformed Munich into a brilliant intellectual and artistic centre, but his affair with dancer and actress Lola Montez greatly contributed to his loss of popularity. He was to abdicate in 1848.*

Drawing inspired by the painting by J.J.F. Langenhöffel, representing Princess ***Augusta-Wilhelmine of Hesse-Darmstadt****, wife of* ***Maximilien****, Count Palatine of Zweibrücken (later* ***King Maximilien I of Bavaria****) with her children Ludwig and Augusta Amalia Ludovika*

In the background is the mirror in question, the work of Jean-Jacques Kirstein

A commemorative plaque on the façade of the Palais du Gouverneur *facing the Place Broglie*

About ***Maximilien-Joseph, Duke of Zweibrücken*** (1756-1825), Baroness Oberkirch wrote:

*" Every Sunday after parade, Prince Max de Deux-Ponts, colonel of the Alsatian regiment, set out for Ollwillon (sic), accompanied by several of his officers, and remained there until Monday. All the resident nobility was invited to meet him and the festivities were on a more than usual scale. They had the reputation of playing for very high stakes on these occasions. Prince Max is very extravagant: King Louis XVI has paid his debts, but he is constantly contracting new ones. He is what is called a "*bon vivant*", delighting in hunting and the pleasures of the table – and, scandal has it, seeks the company of chorus girls. His manners however are dignified and elegant, equally suited for a court or a private drawing room."*

ACKNOWLEDGEMENTS

I wish to thank Monsieur Etienne Martin, Chief Heritage Curator in charge of the Museum of Decorative Arts, for his most valuable advice and for facilitating access to the museum's photographic resources; Madame Catherine Paulus, of the documentation and iconography department, for preparing the photos; the education department for organizing the visits; Monsieur Jean-Marc Marcoux du Trémoul de la Tronchère for photographing the apartments.

Thanks are also due to Monsieur Damien Schitter, graphic designer, whose creativity contributed greatly to the realization of this project.

Lastly, my thanks go also to Mr Richard Tanner, who was kind enough to revise the English text and put the finishing touches to it.

Bibliography

Histoire de Strasbourg des origines à nos jours, Tome II - Georges Livet et Francis Rapp, Strasbourg, Istra, 1981

Le Palais Rohan de Strasbourg, Tome I et II, Jean-Daniel Ludmann, Strasbourg, Istra, 1980

Le Palais Rohan, Etienne Martin, Marc Walter, Editions des Musées de la Ville de Strasbourg, 2012

Deux siècles d'orfèvrerie à Strasbourg, Etienne Martin, Editions des Musées de la Ville de Strasbourg, 2004

Catalogue d'exposition *Le Goût chinois du cardinal Louis de Rohan*. Les collections extrême-orientales du musée des Arts décoratifs, Etienne Martin, Palais Rohan, 2008-2009

Le siècle des Rohan, Claude Muller, Editions La Nuée Bleue, Strasbourg, 2006

Les Empereurs romains, Chris Scarre, Thames & Hudson, 2012

Encyclopédie de l'Art, Garzanti, 1986